POCKET

The Queen

WISDOM

POCKET
The Queen
WISDOM

Inspirational quotes
and wise words
from an iconic monarch

hardie grant books

Pocket The Queen Wisdom

Published in 2018 by Hardie Grant Books,
an imprint of Hardie Grant Publishing

Hardie Grant Books (London)
5th & 6th Floors
52–54 Southwark Street
London SE1 1UN

Hardie Grant Books (Melbourne)
Building 1, 658 Church Street
Richmond, Victoria 3121

hardiegrantbooks.com

British Library Cataloguing-in-Publication Data. A
catalogue record for this book is available from the
British Library.

ISBN: 978-1-78488-225-9

Publisher: Kate Pollard
Senior Editor: Molly Ahuja
Publishing Assistant: Eila Purvis
Design: Daisy Dudley
Illustrator: Michele Rosenthal
Images on pages 7, 31, 55, 65, 75, 91 © Shutterstock

Colour Reproduction by p2d
Printed and bound in China by Leo Paper Group

Contents

The Queen on

LIFE

"

Grief is the price

we pay for

LOVE.

"

"

[On her job] It's all to do with the training: you can do a lot if you're properly trained.

"

"

I know of no single formula
for **SUCCESS**.
But over the years I have
observed that some
attributes of leadership are
universal and are often
about finding ways of…

encouraging people
to combine their efforts,
their talents, their insights,
their enthusiasm and
their inspiration to

WORK
TOGETHER.

"

"

When life seems hard,
the courageous do not lie down
and accept defeat; instead,
they are all the more determined
to struggle for a better future.

"

"

Let us not take ourselves too
seriously. None of us has
a monopoly on wisdom and we
must always be ready to listen and
respect other points of view.

"

"

May you be **PROUD** to remember – as I am myself – how much depends on you, and that even when your life seems most monotonous, what you do is always of real **VALUE** and importance to your fellow men.

"

"

The true measure
of all our actions is how
long the **GOOD** in
them lasts.

"

"

We can make sense
of the future, if we
understand the lessons
of the past.

"

"

The world is not the most pleasant place. Eventually your parents leave you and nobody is going to go out of their way to protect you…

unconditionally. You need to learn to stand up for yourself and what you believe and sometimes – pardon my language – **KICK SOME ASS**.

"

"

Work is the rent
you pay for the room
you occupy on earth.

"

"

In tomorrow's

world we must all

WORK

TOGETHER

as hard as ever.

"

"

It has always been easy

to hate and

DESTROY.

To build and to

CHERISH

is much more difficult.

"

"

Today we need a special
kind of courage. Not the
kind needed in battle, but
a kind which makes us
stand up for everything
we know is right.

"

"

It is possible to have too
much of a good thing.

"

66

I hope we will all be

reminded of the

POWER

of togetherness and the

convening strength of

FAMILY,

friendship and good

neighbourliness.

99

"

There are long periods
when life seems a small,
dull round, a petty business
with no point, and then
suddenly we are caught up…

in some great event,
which gives us a glimpse
of the solid and durable
foundations of our

EXISTENCE.

"

"

GOOD MEMORIES

are our second

chance at

HAPPINESS.

"

"

For me,

HEAVEN

is likely to be a bit

of a come-down.

"

SOCIETY

The Queen on

"

[After 9/11]
My thoughts and
prayers are with you all
now, and in the difficult
days ahead.

"

"

[When a businessman's phone rang as he was speaking to the Queen] Why don't you answer that? It might be someone important.

"

"

We all need to get the
balance right between
action and reflection.
With so many
distractions, it is easy
to forget to pause and
take stock.

"

"

It has been

WOMEN

who have breathed

gentleness and

CARE

into the hard progress

of mankind.

"

"

In the modern world the
opportunities for women
to give something of value to the
human family are greater than
ever, because, through their own
efforts, they are now beginning
to play their full part in public life.

"

"

There can be no doubt,
of course, that

CRITICISM

is good for people and
institutions that are part
of public life.

"

"
TRUE
PATRIOTISM

doesn't exclude an

understanding of the

patriotism of others.

"

"

The lessons from the

PEACE

PROCESS

are clear; whatever life

throws at us…

our individual responses
will be all the stronger for

WORKING

TOGETHER

and sharing the load.

"

"

Let us set out to build
a truer knowledge
of ourselves and our fellow
men to work for tolerance and
understanding among the…

nations and to use the tremendous forces of science and learning for the betterment of man's lot upon this earth.

99

66

The upward course
of a nation's history is
due in the long run to the

SOUNDNESS
OF HEART

of its average men
and women.

99

"

With the benefit of

HISTORICAL

HINDSIGHT

we can all see things

which we would

wish had been differently

or not at all.

"

"

The decisions we make should always be designed to enlarge their [the young's] horizons and enrich their future, from caring for our environment to preventing conflict.

"

"

All of you, near
or far, have been

UNITED

in one purpose.

"

"

The

BRITISH

constitution has always been

PUZZLING

and always will be.

"

66

It is not the new
inventions which are the
difficulty. The trouble
is caused by unthinking
people who carelessly
throw away ageless ideas
as if they were old and
outworn machinery.

99

"

FOOTBALL IS A DIFFICULT BUSINESS

and aren't they

prima donnas?

"

66

1992 is not a year on
which I shall look back
with undiluted pleasure.
In the words of one of my
more sympathetic
correspondents, it has
turned out to be an
annus horribilis.

99

"

[Speaking to Eric
Clapton at a Buckingham
Palace reception in 2005]
Have you been playing
a long time?

"

The Queen on
FAMILY

"

Family does not necessarily

mean blood relatives,

but often a description

of a community,

organisation or nation.

"

"

Like all the best families,
we have our share of
eccentricities, of impetuous and

WAYWARD
YOUNGSTERS

and of family disagreements.

"

"

First, I want to pay tribute
to Diana myself. She was an
exceptional and gifted human
being. In good times and bad,
she never lost her capacity to
smile and laugh, nor to inspire…

others with her warmth and kindness. I admired and respected her – for her energy and commitment to others, and especially for her devotion to her two boys.

99

"

[On Diana]
I, for one, believe there
are lessons to be drawn
from her life and
from the extraordinary
and moving reaction
to her death.

"

"

If I am asked what
I think about family life
after 25 years of

MARRIAGE,

I can answer with equal
simplicity and conviction,
I am for it.

"

"

It's the

SECRET

of a happy marriage to

have different

INTERESTS.

"

"

These wretched

BABIES

don't come until

they are ready.

"

The Queen on

PRINCE PHILIP

66

The Duke of Edinburgh has made an invaluable contribution to my life over these past 50 years, as he has to so many charities and organisations with which he has been involved.

99

"

I think

PRINCE

PHILIP

is

MAD.

"

"

During these years as your Queen, the support of my family has, across the generations, been beyond measure. Prince Philip is, I believe, well-known for…

declining compliments
of any kind. But throughout
he has been a

CONSTANT
STRENGTH

and guide.

99

"

Philip once met an Australian man who said: 'My wife is a doctor of philosophy and much more important than I am.' Philip said 'Ah yes, we have that trouble in our family too.'

"

66

He has quite simply been

MY STRENGTH

and stay all these years,

and I and his whole family…

and this and many other countries owe him a debt greater than he would ever claim or we shall ever know.

"

The Queen on
HERSELF

"

I have in

SINCERITY

PLEDGED

MYSELF...

to your service

as so many of you are

PLEDGED TO

MINE.

"

"

I simply ache from
smiling. Why are

WOMEN
EXPECTED
TO BEAM

all the time…

It's **UNFAIR**.
If a man looks solemn,
it's automatically
assumed he's
a serious person,
not a miserable one.

,,

66

I don't like to badmouth
people. But I'm the head of a
monarchy that began in the
ninth century, and I'm
apparently more modern than
Chris Christie. Look, I know…

he has to appeal to the crazy right-wingers in his party, but the fact is, he's not as forward-thinking as an eighty-seven-year-old lady who wears a crown on her head. It's pathetic.

99

"

[I should]
like to be a lady,
living in the

COUNTRY

with lots of

HORSES

and dogs.

"

"

I cannot lead you into battle. **I DO NOT** give you laws or **ADMINISTER JUSTICE,** but I can do something else…

I can

GIVE MY

HEART

and my devotion to these
old islands and to all the
peoples of our brotherhood
of nations.

,,

"

I declare before you all
that my whole life,
whether it be long or
short, shall be devoted to
your service and the
service of our great
Imperial family to which
we all belong.

"

"

I have to be

SEEN

to be

BELIEVED.

"

"

It is inevitable that
I should seem a rather

REMOTE
FIGURE

to many of you.
A successor to the
Kings and Queens...

of history; someone whose face may be familiar in newspaper and films but who never really touches your

PERSONAL LIVES.

"

12

Facts on
The Queen

The Queen's full title in the United Kingdom
is: Elizabeth II, by the Grace of God,
of the United Kingdom of Great Britain and
Northern Ireland, and of her other Realms
and Territories Queen, Head of the
Commonwealth, Defender of the Faith.

She's been wearing the same nail polish since
1989 – *Essie*'s Ballet Slippers.

The Queen used to own two sloths, which were
given to her during a state visit to Brazil in 1968.

4

The Queen is the only person in the UK who doesn't need a driver's license or a license plate to drive. Or even a passport to travel internationally.

5

Her favourite cake is honey and cream sponge.

6

She has owned over 30 corgis.
Her first dog was named Susan.

Every morning for breakfast, the Queen
is served cornflakes and porridge oats
in Tupperware containers, yoghurt and two
varieties of marmalade – light and dark.

The Queen speaks fluent French so well that she
doesn't need a translator.

The Queen bred one of her corgi's with Princess
Margaret's dachshund, creating the first 'dorgi'.
There have been 8 dorgis.

The Queen and her sister, Princess Margaret, once partied incognito in the streets of London.

The Queen drinks a glass of Champagne every night before bed.

She can imitate the sound of a Concorde jet landing.

Sources

Angela Bell, 6th July 2016 - p. **82**

Alan Titchmarsh (2013) *Elizabeth: Her Life, Our Times*, Random House – pp. **24, 35, 36, 37**

BBC, 7th July 2010 – p. **21**

CBC News, 25th June 2010 – pp. **12, 25, 52, 53, 72–73, 84–85, 86**

Economist, 25th June 2009 – p. **48**

Financial Times, 9th March 2015 – p. **29**

Guardian, 24th December 2017 – pp. **42–43**

Harpers Bazaar, 20th November 2017 – pp. **61, 66, 68–69**

Huffington Post, 22nd May 2015 – pp. **9, 51, 63, 87**

Ingrid Seward (2015) *The Queen's Speech: An Intimate Portrait of the Queen in her Own Words*, Simon and Schuster – pp. **16, 17, 46**

Independent, 4th February 2012 – pp. **33, 57**

Insider, 5th June 2018– pp. **92, 93, 94, 95**

International Business Times, 25th December 2013 – p. **34**

International Business Times, 20th April 2016 – pp. **28, 38, 78–79**

International Business Times, 21st April 2017 – pp. **10–11, 18–19, 80–81**

Irish Times, 18th May 2011 – pp. **40–41**

Royal, 2nd June 1953 – pp. **47, 76–77**

Royal, 25th December 1957 – pp. **50, 88–89**

Royal, 25th December 1991 – p. **13**

Royal, 25th December 1994 – pp. **14, 22, 23, 44**

Royal, 25th January 2018 – pp. **92, 94**

Royal Central, 21st April 2018 – pp. **92, 93, 94**

Sally Bedell Smith (2012) *Elizabeth the Queen: The real story behind The Crown*, Penguin UK – pp. **26–27**

Telegraph, 6th September 1997 – pp. **28, 58–59, 60**

Telegraph, 21st September 2001 – pp. **8, 32**

Telegraph, 1st April 2001 – p. **20**

Telegraph, 18th May 2011 – p. **45**

Telegraph, 24th December 2017 – p. **56**

WSFM, 21st April 2016 – pp. **28**

Vogue, 4th May 2017 – pp. **62, 67, 70**